THIS IS A BORZOI BOOK PUBLISHED BY ALFRED A. KNOPF, INC.
Copyright © 1999 by Richard Burnie

All rights reserved under International and Pan-American Copyright
Conventions. Published in the United States by Alfred A. Knopf, Inc., New
York, and simultaneously in Canada by Random House of Canada Limited,
Toronto. Distributed by Random House, Inc., New York. Originally
published in Great Britain in 1999 by Jonathan Cape,
a division of Random House UK Limited.

www.randomhouse.com/kids

*Library of Congress Cataloging-in-Publication Data*
Burnie, Richard.
Monumental mazes / by Richard Burnie.
p. cm.
Summary: A series of mazes and games in such historical settings
as the Crimean War and ancient Egypt.
ISBN 0-375-80155-3
1. Maze puzzles—Juvenile literature. [1. Maze puzzles. 2. Puzzles.] I. Title.
II. Title: Monumental mazes.
GV1507.M3B87
1999
793.73'8—dc21
98-49317

Printed in Singapore

10 9 8 7 6 5 4 3 2 1

First American edition: 1999

# MONUMENTAL MAZES

# MONUMENTAL MAZES

## RICHARD BURNIE

ALFRED A. KNOPF
NEW YORK

MANHATTAN SKYSCRAPER
After working late on the steel framework of a new
building, a riveter finds himself alone on the site. How can
he get to the elevator—climbing up, down, and along the
girders—without setting foot on the level below, which is
patrolled by guard dogs?

## VENICE

There are six cafés on the flooded piazza in Venice, and they have very few customers. Starting and finishing at the café at the top left, the one and only waiter visits each café in a clockwise direction. He must avoid colliding with other pedestrians on the temporary walkways, which would make him spill the drinks on his tray. Can you find a route for him? Can you also find a dog, a sailboat, a guitar, and a clock?

THE GREAT WALL OF CHINA
The imperial party needs to take a detour around a crumbled
section of the Great Wall. They must avoid the local farmers,
who deal roughly with trespassers who trample their crops.
Find a safe path for His Royal Highness to follow.

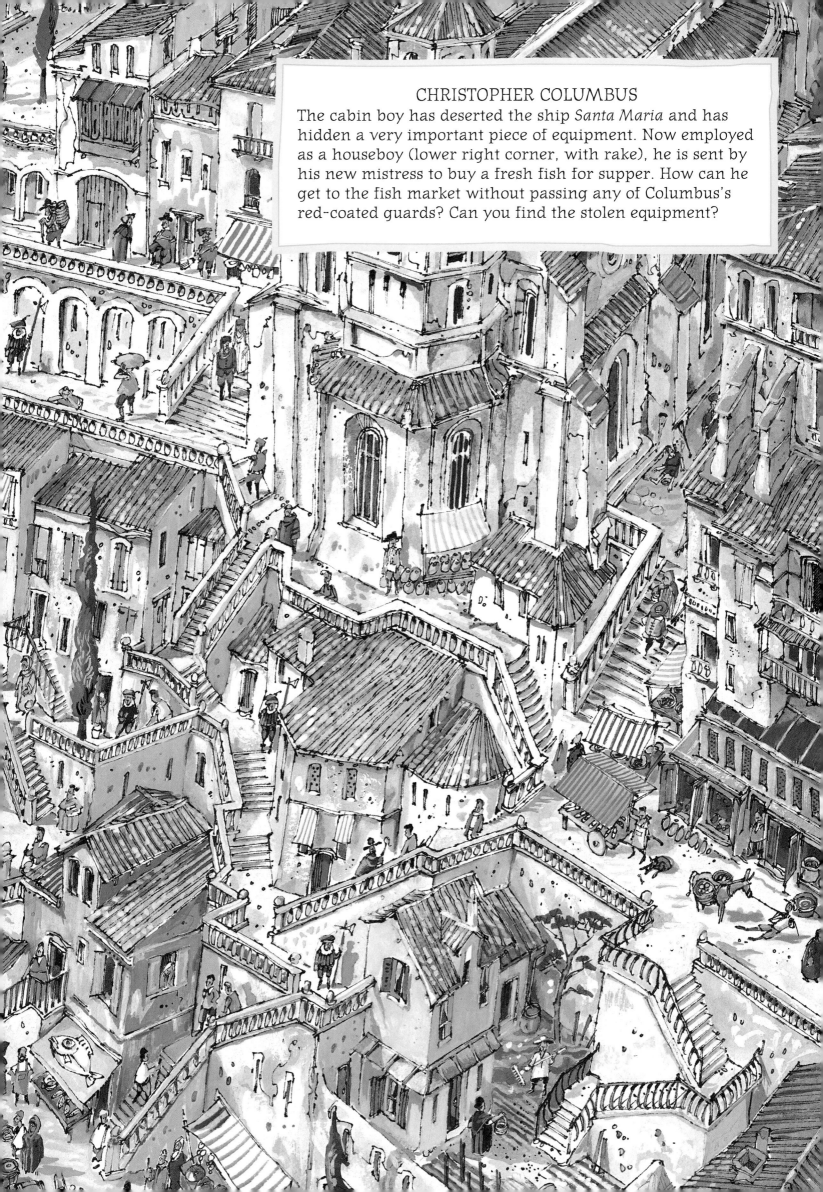

CHRISTOPHER COLUMBUS
The cabin boy has deserted the ship *Santa Maria* and has hidden a very important piece of equipment. Now employed as a houseboy (lower right corner, with rake), he is sent by his new mistress to buy a fresh fish for supper. How can he get to the fish market without passing any of Columbus's red-coated guards? Can you find the stolen equipment?

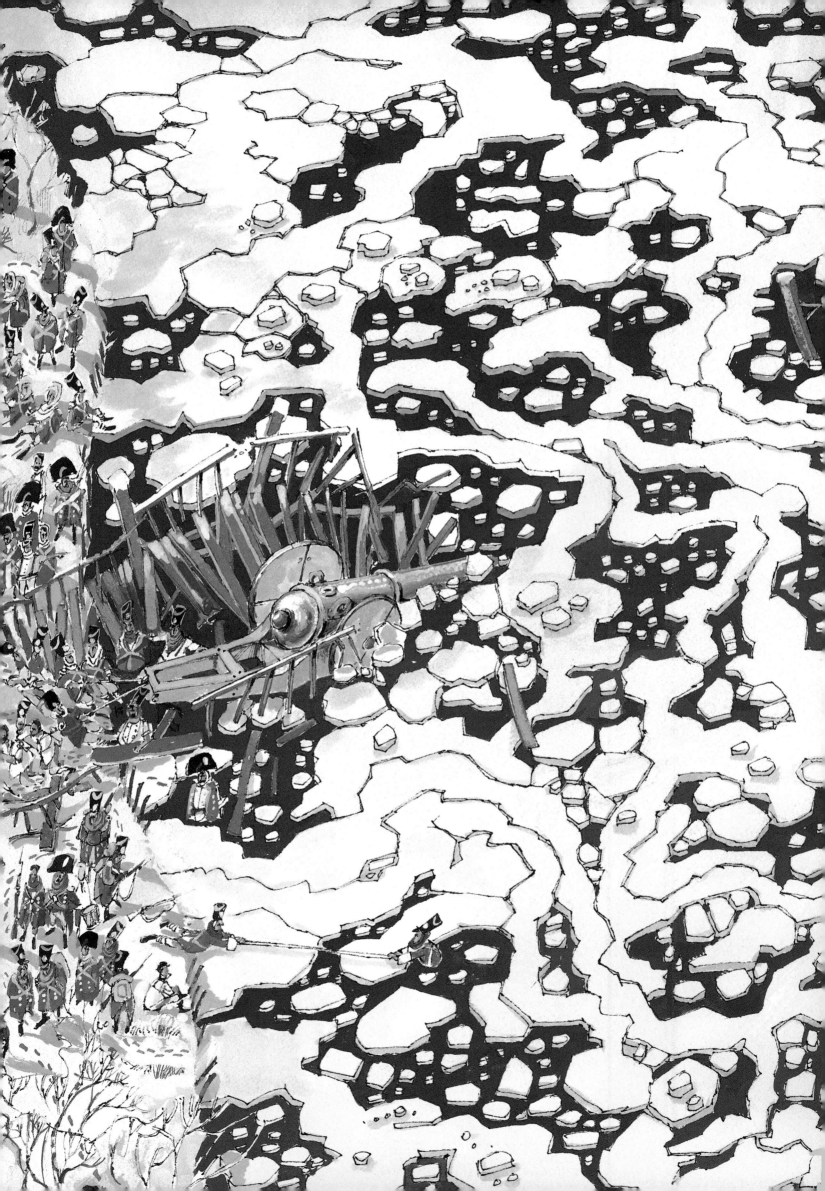

## THE GREAT RETREAT FROM MOSCOW
Napoleon's army, retreating from Moscow, has collapsed the bridge across the River Neman with the great weight of their cannon. Starting from the riverbank, they must find a route to the far bank without crossing any cracks or gaps in the ice.

### THE MOGUL TEMPLE
Souvenir hunters are dismantling the Mogul Temple. Can you find ten giant tools used by these vandals to carry out the demolition? Can you spot one of the vandals making off with his prize?

## THE LADY WITH THE LAMP

Woken at dawn by the sounds of a party, Florence Nightingale must silence the revelers. Since she must be careful to avoid the rooms of sleeping soldiers, what route will she take?

THE ROMAN ARENA
To escape through the exit at the far right, the sweeper can climb up the steps and seats of the arena—but he must not step over any sleeping gladiators or run into any of the escaping lions. Which route will he take? Can you find the giant lock and key that would have kept the lions in their cage?

## THE EIFFEL TOWER
The Eiffel Tower in Paris is one of the biggest and most dangerous structures in the world to paint. Without climbing over the fresh red undercoat, how can the workman rescue his unfortunate colleague?

THE CHATEAU ON THE LOIRE
King Louis XIV's prize herd of pedigree cows have broken loose and are wreaking havoc in the gardens. The cow at the top of the maze must join the cows in the center, and then all four cows must get out of the maze. Can you find their routes? Can you round up ten other cows?

ANCIENT EGYPT
On the Great Sphinx, a daring slave makes a break for freedom. He must get down off the giant statue without passing any of the slave drivers. Can you find a path for him? Can you find his waiting desert transportation?

# SOLUTIONS

## MANHATTAN SKYSCRAPER

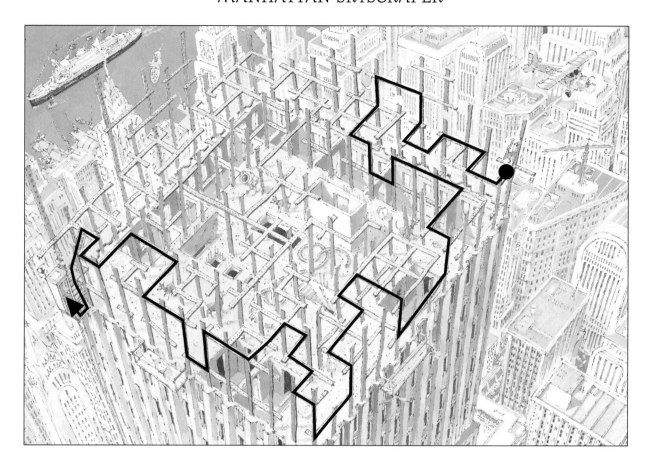

## VENICE

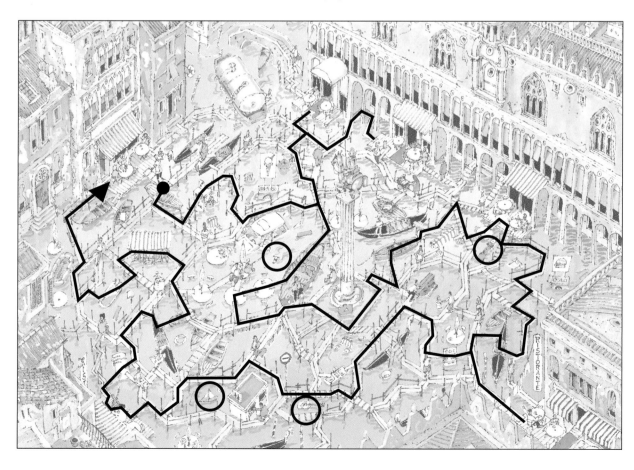

# THE GREAT WALL OF CHINA

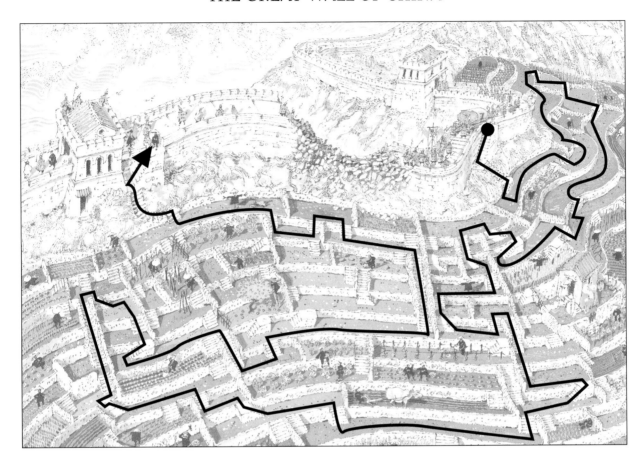

# CHRISTOPHER COLUMBUS

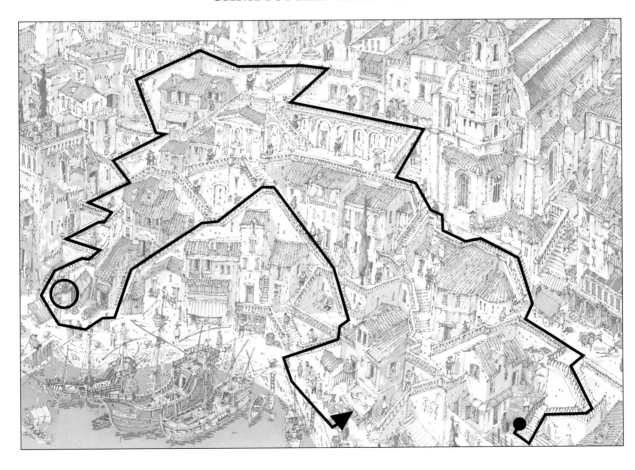

# THE GREAT RETREAT FROM MOSCOW

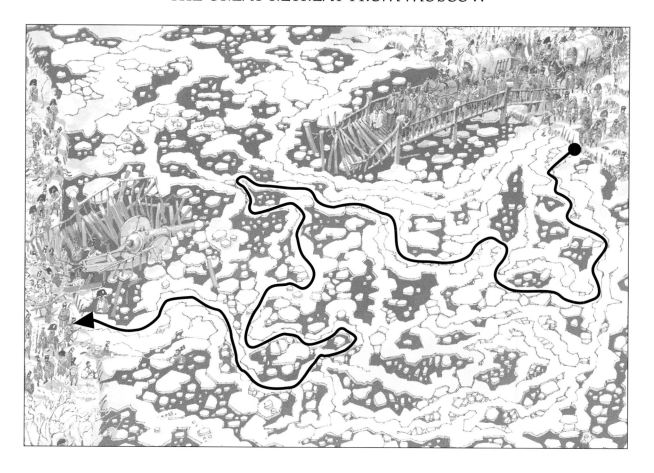

# THE MOGUL TEMPLE

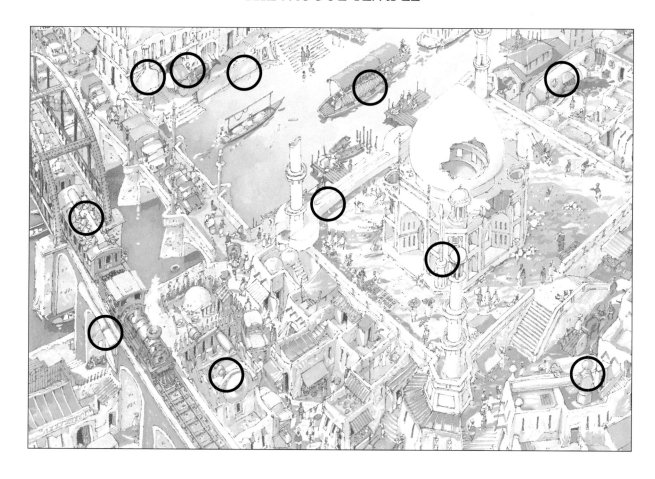

# THE LADY WITH THE LAMP

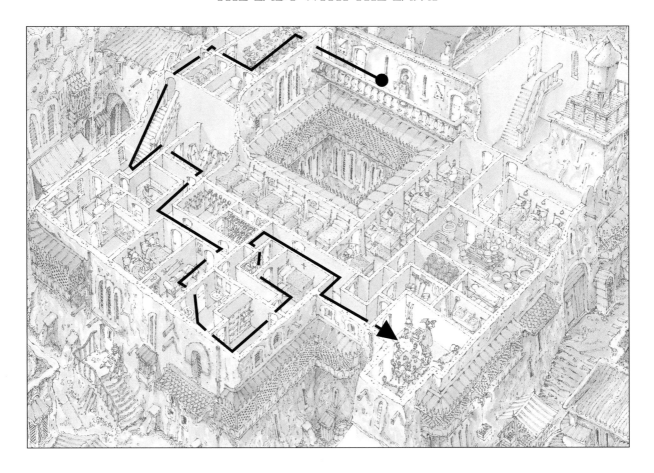

# THE ROMAN ARENA

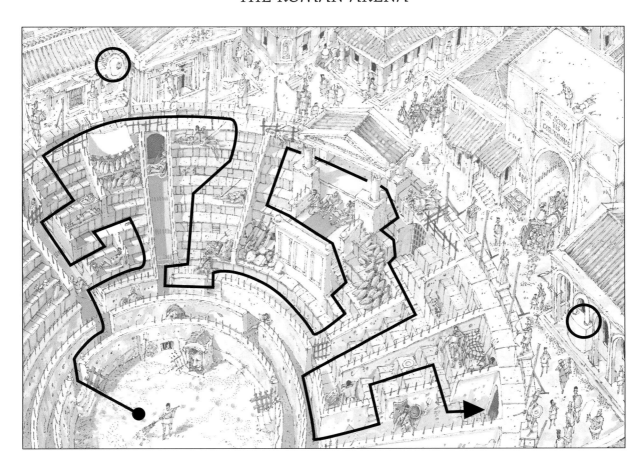

# THE EIFFEL TOWER

# THE CHATEAU ON THE LOIRE

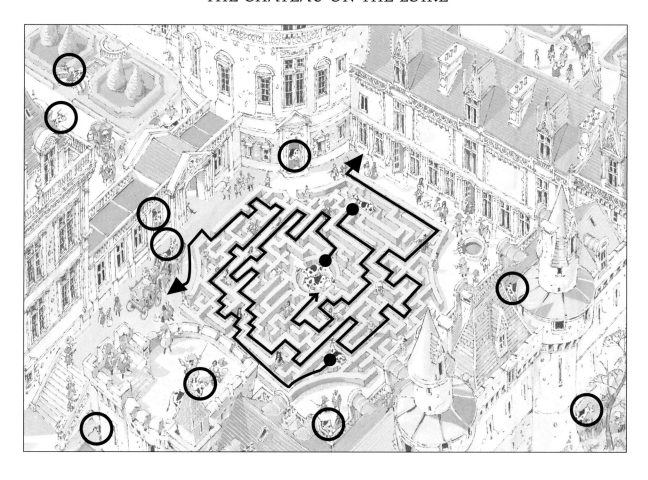

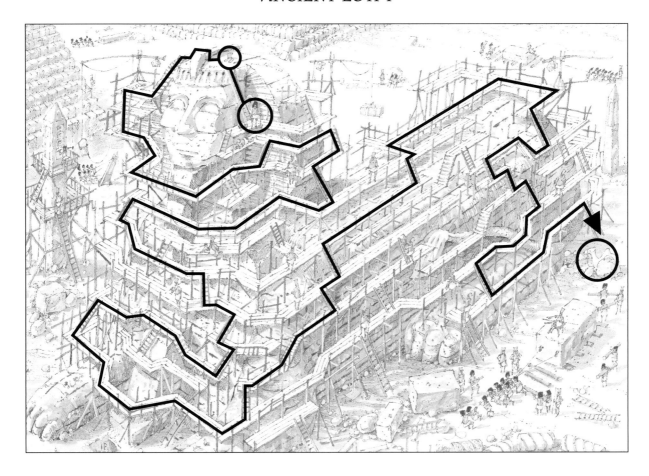

## MANHATTAN SKYSCRAPER

The first skyscraper was built in Chicago in the 1880s, and by the 1920s, with advances in construction techniques, they became widespread. New York City boasts the most spectacular concentration of skyscrapers in the world. The builders of Manhattan's first skyscrapers were called "girder gorillas," as they climbed about the frameworks at astounding heights.

## VENICE

Venice was founded in A.D. 452 on low-lying islands in the Adriatic Sea, an arm of the Mediterranean. Instead of streets, canals run through the city, and Venetians travel by gondolas and other boats instead of cars. Venice is at the mercy of the tides and its slowly sinking foundation, and is flooded regularly. Residents must build temporary walkways over what are usually sidewalks.

## THE GREAT WALL OF CHINA

The Great Wall of China is the longest man-made structure in the world. Built to keep out invaders, the wall extends 4,000 miles, from the Yellow Sea to the mountains of Tibet. Sections of the wall were built as early as 210 B.C. and as recently as only 500 years ago.

## CHRISTOPHER COLUMBUS

In 1492, in search of a new trade route to Asia, Columbus's three small ships—the *Niña*, the *Pinta*, and the *Santa Maria*—sailed westward from Spain across the Atlantic. Columbus made his first landfall in what is now the Bahamas, and later went on to discover the mainland of North America.

## THE GREAT RETREAT FROM MOSCOW

Having made the fateful decision to invade Russia in 1812, the French Emperor Napoleon Bonaparte was forced to retreat, defeated both by the Russians and by the bitter Russian winter. Half a million French soldiers died of cold or starvation, deserted, or were captured during the invasion and retreat, and only a handful made it back to France through the awful conditions.

## THE MOGUL TEMPLE

In India, the banks of the sacred Ganges River are crowded with ancient Hindu temples from the Mogul Empire, which ruled most of India in the 1500s and 1600s. The Taj Mahal, the most famous temple from the Mogul Empire, stands in Agra, India. It was built between 1630 and 1650 by an Indian ruler as a tomb for his favorite wife.

## THE LADY WITH THE LAMP

In 1854, appalled by reports of the suffering of British soldiers wounded while fighting the Russians in the Crimean War, Florence Nightingale took a team of nurses to the Barrack Hospital in Scutari, Turkey. Through her efforts, she reduced the hospital death rate greatly. She was the founder of nursing as a profession, and the lamp she carried on her nightly rounds became a symbol of the care and relief she brought to the wounded.

## THE ROMAN ARENA

Arenas, like Rome's famous Colosseum, were the venue for a bloodthirsty mix of sport, combat, and theater, where gladiators often battled to the death. These ampitheaters were most popular between the years 200 B.C. and A.D. 400, and were found throughout the Roman Empire.

## THE EIFFEL TOWER

The unmistakable outline of the Eiffel Tower has dominated the skyline of Paris for more than a century. It was built in 1889 to commemorate the Paris Exposition. The iron-and-steel structure is 984 feet tall.

## THE CHATEAU ON THE LOIRE

The sixty or so chateaux that line the banks of the river Loire south of Paris were built beginning in the 1500s as country residences for French royalty and nobility. The owners of these extravagant dwellings were constantly striving to outdo each other.

## ANCIENT EGYPT

A sphinx is a mythological creature, usually depicted with the body of a lion and the head of a human. The Great Sphinx, in Giza, Egypt, is 240 feet long and 66 feet high, and was carved from limestone about 4,500 years ago. The exact purpose of the Sphinx remains a mystery, though perhaps it was built to honor a king or queen.